SO-BJN-618

# Cleaning the House

John Malam

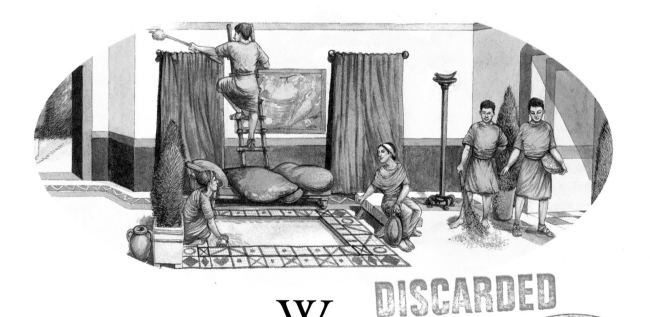

W
# FRANKLIN WATTS
A Division of Grolier Publishing
NEW YORK • LONDON • HONG KONG • SYDNEY
DANBURY, CONNECTICUT

First published in 2000 by Franklin Watts
Copyright © Franklin Watts 1999

First American edition 2000 by
Franklin Watts/Children's Press
A Division of Grolier Publishing
90 Sherman Turnpike
Danbury, CT 06816

Library of Congress Cataloging-in-Publication Data
Malam, John.
  Cleaning the house / John Malam
    p.cm. -- (Everyday history)
  Includes bibliographical references and index.
  Summary: Describes how people have handled household tasks such as dusting, sweeping, and trash disposal since the Stone Age and discusses the invention of such cleaning items as the vacuum cleaner and dishwasher, the discovery of soap, and more.
  ISBN 0-531-14553-0 (hbk)
     0-531-15411-4 (pbk)
    1.. House cleaning--Juvenile literature. [1. House cleaning.] I. Title. II Series.

TX324 .M36 2000
648'5--dc21                    99-046833

GROLIER
PUBLISHING

Visit Franklin Watts/Children's Press on the Internet at:
http://publishing.grolier.com

Printed in Malaysia

Planning and production by Discovery Books Limited
Editors: Gianna Williams, Samantha Armstrong
Design: Ian Winton
Art Director: Jonathan Hair
Illustrators: Kevin Maddison, Pamela Goodchild, Stefan Chabluk
**Photographs:** 4 J. Wright/Hutchison Library, 5 Charles Tait/ Ancient Art & Architecture, 6 G. Tortoli/Ancient Art & Architecture, 9 R. Sheridan/Ancient Art & Architecture, 11 The Makins Collection/Bridgeman Art Library, 12 Mary Evans Picture Library, 13 top Advertising Archives, 13 bottom Beamish Photographic Archive, 15 top Whitford & Hughes, London/Bridgeman Art Library, 15 bottom & 16 Robert Opie Collection, 19 top Musee des Beaux Arts, Rouen/Bridgeman Art Library, 19 bottom Mary Evans Picture Library, 20 top Mary Evans Picture Library, 20 bottom Discovery Picture Library, 21 top Robert Opie Collection, 21 bottom Ferens Art Gallery/Bridgeman Art Library, 22 top Robert Opie Collection, 22 bottom Adam Gallery/Bridgeman Art Library, 24 top Discovery Picture Library, 24 bottom Beamish Photographic Archive, 25 top Mary Evans Picture Library, 25 bottom Advertising Archives, 26 top Robert Opie Collection, 26 bottom & 27 Advertising Archives, 28 top Thomas Buchholz/ Bruce Coleman Collection, 29 Michael Macintyre/ Hutchison Library.
**Acknowledgements:** Franklin Watts would like to thank Johnson's Cleaners for the loan of material.

# Contents

# The First Houses

A house is a building in which people live. It can be anything from a hut with one room to a palace with hundreds of rooms. The world's first houses were built about 11,000 years ago. Before that time, people had no need for houses because they were nomads, who wandered across the land, never staying long in any one place.

▲ Present-day nomads, like these Bedouin from North Africa, live in tents.

## Ancient Garbage

As people settled down and began living in houses, they began to create garbage as they went about their everyday lives. Clay pots got broken; bones, shells, and vegetable waste from food preparation lay on the ground, as did pieces of wood and fragments of stone.

Early humans buried their garbage in pits.

# Skara Brae

Skara Brae is a 5,000-year-old village on the island of Orkney, just off the north coast of Scotland. Its round houses are built from stone and linked by narrow passages. Inside, slabs of flat stone were used to make fireplaces, beds, and cupboards. The villagers lived on shellfish, cattle, sheep, and eggs. We know this because bones and shells were dumped into garbage middens between the houses. The middens were piled up against the walls of the houses, and some were on the roofs.

## Cleaning the House

We can't be certain how the first houses were cleaned, but archaeologists often find pits dug into the ground, filled with pieces of broken pottery and animal bones. This suggests the occupants of the houses buried their garbage and tried to keep their houses clean. Sometimes there was too much garbage to bury, so it was heaped up into mounds, called middens.

# In Ancient Times

Some of the world's first houses were built in Mesopotamia (an area in the Middle East). The remains of an 8,000-year-old mud-brick town have been found at Çatal Hüyük. It had as many as 1,000 houses, packed so closely together that there were no streets between them.

A huge mound of broken mud bricks is all that remains today of Çatal Hüyük.

## Houses in Çatal Hüyük

Most houses had two rooms — a large one for everyday living and a smaller one for storage. The main room had hardened clay benches or platforms (which may have been for sleeping on), fireplaces, and ovens. The way into a house was through a hole in the roof. The hole was above the fireplace and was also used as a chimney.

# Cleaning Floors

The floor was made from beaten earth and may have been covered with mats of woven reeds and grass. Perhaps people used brushes made from reeds or dried grass to sweep the dusty floors. These houses must have been difficult to clean because garbage had to be taken out through the hole in the roof. From time to time the floors were dug up, not because they were dirty or worn out, but because people were buried inside their own homes.

Houses in Çatal Hüyük were built so closely together, people walked on the roofs.

# Greeks and Romans

The Greeks and Romans built houses from stone, wood, tile, and brick. Servants and slaves cared for the houses of the wealthy, while the poor did their own housework. It was a woman's duty to clean the house.

▲ A housewife in ancient Greece begins her daily chores.

## A Greek Home

Greek houses were usually built around a courtyard with a well. Downstairs, floors were made of hard-packed earth, cement, or pebbles. Upstairs, floors were made of wood. Woolen rugs and reed mats were laid over the floors, though the poorest houses had no floor coverings at all. Rugs and mats could be taken outside and shaken clean or beaten with sticks.

# Roman Waterworks

Cleaning the house is much easier when there is a water supply close by. Roman towns were supplied with water through underground channels and aqueducts. The water was then brought into houses by lead pipes. At the same time, Roman cities had drainage and sewage systems, as well as public toilets and baths, to help make sure that the town stayed clean and healthy.

## Housework in Rome

At sunrise in the house of a wealthy Roman, a bell rang. It called the servants to their daily duties. They were armed with buckets, cloths, ladders to reach the ceilings, poles with sponges attached to the ends, feather dusters, and brooms. Their brooms were made of green palms or twigs from tamarisk trees, heather, and myrtle twisted together. They scattered sawdust over the floors, then swept it off along with the dirt.

# Town and Country

Between A.D. 500 and 1500, towns in medieval Europe were mazes of narrow streets lined with wooden buildings. They were dirty places. Garbage and animal bones were thrown into pits at the back of the buildings, though it was often simpler to throw them into the street.

## A Country Cottage

Medieval cottages were small, cramped places. People owned very little furniture. There were no glass windows, just openings covered with wooden shutters or oiled parchment.

Medieval streets were little more than open sewers.

## Garderobes

Castles and large houses had rooms called garderobes. They were often built next to bedrooms, and were used as a bathroom. They had an open shaft, down which garbage and waste was thrown. The shaft emptied into a river, moat, or sewage pit called a cesspit.

## Chimneys and Fireplaces

Medieval houses had no chimneys, so smoke from open fires left sooty dust everywhere. Inside, walls were brightened up with a light-colored lime wash. When it wore off, a new coat was brushed on. After about 1500, houses had chimneys built above fireplaces, which drew smoke straight out of the buildings.

## Straw Floors

In many poor houses, floors were made from beaten soil, sometimes with pebbles rammed into them to make them hard wearing. To keep floors warm and dry, householders covered them with loose rushes or straw. When the floor became dirty, the housewife threw another layer of straw down.

The interior of a peasant's cottage in the 1600s.

Over time, the straw rotted and was trampled into the floor. This made clearing out the old straw a difficult job that was only done once or twice a year, and sometimes even less often.

# Discovering Germs

Living conditions did not change for many centuries. Then, during the 1800s, the population of towns increased at a rapid pace. The poor lived in rotten, overcrowded, smelly houses. There was no running water or drainage, so people had no choice but to collect water at wells or pumps and throw wastewater into the streets and rivers. Diseases such as cholera killed many thousands of people.

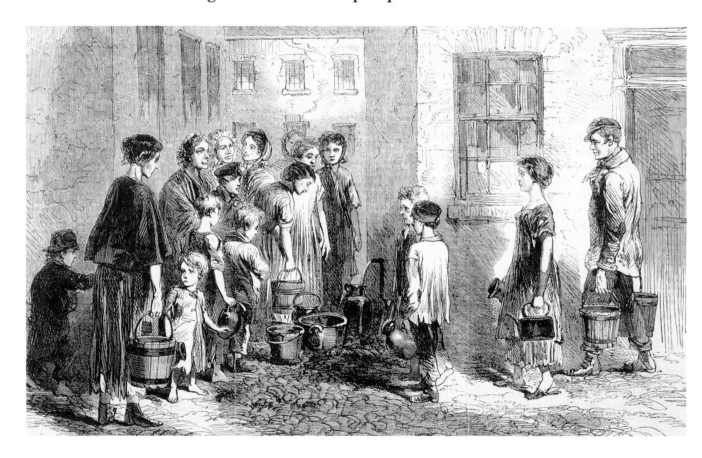

The poor line up for water at a standpipe in the 1860s.

## Germs and Hygiene

However, scientific discoveries about the germs that lived in dirty conditions made town councils realize how important cleanliness was. At the same time, there were many new inventions that helped the fight against germs.

## Disinfectants

In the 1860s, it was discovered that a spray made from carbolic acid killed germs. Manufacturers began making liquid cleaners, or disinfectants, for use in the home. Work surfaces, clothes, and dishes were scrubbed with mixtures of carbolic acid or potassium permanganate.

▶ Advertisements, like this one, appeared in magazines for new cleaning products.

## A Mucky Job

Until the 1840s, town sewage from drains and toilets often went straight into rivers and streams. There were rats and pollution, and diseases spread. After the 1840s, towns built networks of underground sewers. Raw sewage was sent through the sewers to treatment plants. But not all houses were connected to the new sewer pipes. These houses still needed the services of night-soil men, who came at night to take the sewage away in buckets and carts. It was an unpleasant, mucky job.

# Bedbugs and Feather Duster

Bedbugs are blood-sucking insects. These bugs were a constant source of annoyance for householders — rich and poor alike — in the nineteenth century. Homemade mattresses and pillows became infested, and they had to be picked clear of bugs once a year, and the feathers inside exposed to the sun to dry.

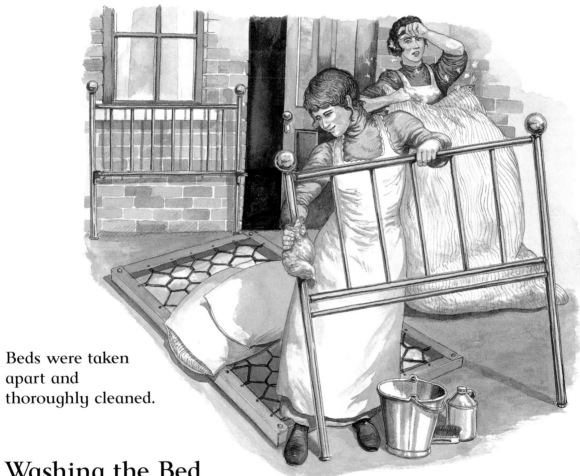

Beds were taken apart and thoroughly cleaned.

## Washing the Bed

One method of removing insects from beds was to take every bed frame in the house apart once a year, and wash the joints with boiling water and soap. If this did not work, housewives or servants washed the bed with kerosene to try to kill the bugs.

## Feather Dusters

For many years, dusters made from feathers were the main means of dusting inside a house. But feather dusters did not pick the dust up. Instead, they just flicked it back up into the air. Dust was constantly being moved around the house from one room to another.

In order to limit the amount of times that furniture needed dusting or cleaning, furniture was often covered with dustcovers when not in use. If a family went away for a few weeks on a vacation, every piece of furniture would be covered up to protect it.

A maid at work with a feather duster in the 1800s.

# Pests in the House

Every house has its share of pests. Some are visitors, others are permanent residents. Flies, moths, fleas, beetles, and cockroaches eat our clothes, food, furniture, and some even suck our blood. Mice and rats love kitchens, pantries and cellars, where we keep our food. These rodents carry germs and diseases that spread to humans, and from the earliest times we have used mousetraps and poison against them.

# A Housemaid's Work

Most work around the house was done by women, and in larger houses it was the housemaids who kept the property clean. Housemaids followed a daily timetable. In the 1870s, a typical servant's day would have begun at six o'clock.

▶ Large houses had many fireplaces to clean every day.

## Cleaning the Fireplace

The first job of the day was to clean the fireplace. After sweeping the floor around the front of it, she removed the fender (a fender stopped burning coal from falling onto the carpet). She scraped the ashes from the fireplace and put them into her cinder pail. Then she polished the iron grate with black lead to make it clean and shiny again.

Black lead was rubbed onto iron fireplaces and kitchen stoves.

## Sweep and Dust

The next job was to sweep the floors, dust, and prepare the downstairs rooms. After dusting, the housemaid opened the windows to air the rooms. She then went around the house, emptying chamber pots into slop buckets, an unpleasant job, and changing the water that was kept in jugs around the house. She would then make the beds, sweep the floors, and dust the upstairs rooms.

Airing the bedroom.

Sweeping floors.

## How to Clean Windows

1. Add two tablespoons of vinegar to half a bottle of tap water. Pour into a plant-spray bottle.

2. Spray onto a window.

3. Wipe the window dry with a crumpled-up page of newspaper.

# Scrubbing and Mopping

From the 1860s onward, fresh water was piped straight in to people's houses. Washing in the house became a much easier job if you didn't have to carry the water home first.

## Water for Floors

In large houses, servants scrubbed floors clean nearly every day, using mops dipped into buckets of water. In many houses, halls and kitchens had tiled floors. These surfaces were easily cleaned, as were rooms with linoleum floors. This hard-wearing material was introduced in the 1860s.

Steps were scrubbed with roughened stones.

## Front Steps

In the days when streets were littered with horse dung and mud, it was important to wash the front steps. They were scrubbed clean with a donkey stone. It contained pieces of fine grit that were rough enough to wear away the surface of the step and remove any dirty marks.

## Water for Dishes

Water was boiled in kettles and poured into stone or copper sinks and tubs. Handheld mops, scouring pads, sponges, and cloths were used to wash dishes, pans, and cutlery.

A kitchen maid washes dishes in the 1870s.

## A Machine to Wash the Dishes

In 1865, L. A. Alexander, an American inventor, came up with the idea of a dishwasher. The plates were stacked into a cradle in a water-filled metal tub. When the handle was turned, the cradle whirled through the water and the dishes were washed. There were many other designs for dishwashers at the time, like this one. But people preferred to use dishcloths and "elbow grease."

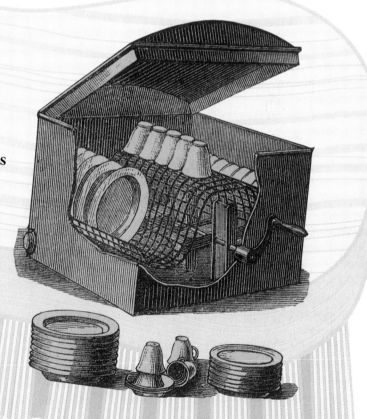

# Laundry Day

In many households in the nineteenth century, Monday was laundry day. Clothes and linens were soaked in soapy water and were then pounded by hand to loosen the dirt. In the 1850s, handheld wooden agitators, or dollies, came into use.

A dolly was twisted up and down inside a wash tub to loosen the dirt.

## Wringing and Drying

After washing, clothes were wrung out by hand; by 1880, wringing machines, called mangles, were used. Clothes were then ready to be dried. Some large houses had drying rooms built with furnaces inside them. In houses without drying rooms, the damp clothes were hung on frames close to the ceiling. Rising warm air from fires and ovens soon dried them.

Wringing machines took the hard work out of squeezing wet clothes.

## Ironing

Finally, heavy flatirons were heated on stoves and then pressed onto clothes and linen, smoothing out unwanted creases. There were several types of flatirons. The simplest were made of solid iron. Others had hollow chambers where slow-burning charcoal was held. From the 1890s, kerosene and oil-fired irons became popular, but all were eventually replaced by the electric iron, which was invented in the United States.

A flatiron with its stand.

## Spring Cleaning

Women often did their biggest household chores in spring. It was a good time because fires did not have to be lit all the time, so there was less soot in the house. Many bugs lay their eggs in spring, so it was good to clean them out too. Everything was scrubbed, from curtains to pictures to floors. The sweep came to clean the chimney. Even today, people spring-clean every year.

# A Polished Home

In nineteenth-century homes, tables, chairs, sideboards, dressers, and bedframes were all made from wood, and they all needed polishing. Furniture polishes could be bought, although many people preferred to make their own out of wax and soap. Beeswax dissolved in turpentine made a wax polish for furniture. If too much wax was applied, the excess could be removed with brick dust sieved through a stocking.

Polish was sold in small tins, like this one.

## A Recipe for Polish

This recipe dates from the 1880s: "Boil a pint (600ml) of soft water, then pour it into a mixing bowl. Let it go cold. Shred into it an ounce (28g) of white wax and an ounce (28g) of yellow soap. Stand the bowl in the oven until all is melted. Take it out and add, gradually, a pint (600ml) of turpentine, stirring until cold. Then bottle and cork the mixture."

# The Boot Boy

Some households employed a boot boy, whose job it was to clean and polish the boots and shoes in the house. But cleaning shoes was not his only job.

Large households had many pairs of boots and shoes.

He might also polish the brass knobs on the front door, and the brass and copper pots and pans in the kitchen. Then coal scuttles kept beside the fireplaces needed filling with coal, and knives needed cleaning and sharpening.

# Sweeping and Sucking

When carpets became cheaper, thanks to mass production in factories from the mid-1800s, they were used to make rooms warmer and cozier. But cleaning them was a heavy, time-consuming job. Carpets were either lifted up and beaten outside with canes or brushed with brooms.

▲ Carpet beaters helped loosen the dirt.

## Brushes for Sweeping

In the 1870s, an American named Melville Bissell invented a machine he called a carpet sweeper. It was a brush on wheels that spun around and around. The new invention was popular with housewives everywhere. Although it didn't sweep up every speck of dust, it was easier than having to take rugs out and beat them.

A late nineteenth-century advertisement for carpet sweepers.

## Electricity for Sucking

An even better machine was invented around 1900 — the vacuum cleaner.

The first vacuum cleaners were huge machines. They were parked in the street and their hoses were fed in through open windows. In 1907, American James Spangler

Early vacuum cleaners were so big, they were parked outside.

from Ohio attached a small electric fan to a broom handle. It sucked dust through a pipe into a pillowcase. Spangler sold his idea to W. H. Hoover, and the following year the first Hoover vacuum cleaners went on sale at $70 each.

## Anti-Macassars

In the nineteenth century, it became very popular for men to wear Macassar oil on their hair. Unfortunately, every time they sat down and rested their heads on a chair or sofa, the oil left a stain that was very difficult to clean. Women protected their furnishings by making "anti-macassars," square pieces of cloth that were draped over the tops of chairs. Today, anti-macassars can still be found, among other places, on airplane seats.

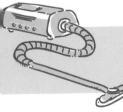

# Cleaning Made Easy

In the twentieth century, new inventions made cleaning the home easier and faster than ever before. During World War I (1914-1918) and World War II (1939-1945), women were encouraged to find new kinds of work outside the home. They had less time to do housework and were eager to try the new cleaning products and inventions.

◀ A 1950s vacuum cleaner.

A World War II poster encourages women to volunteer to help in the war.

## Make a Sticker-Picker

1. Cut some adhesive tape, about 12in (30cm) long.

2. Wind the tape around your palm and fingers (not your thumb), making sure the sticky side is always on the outside.

3. Use the sticker-picker on clothes and furnishings to remove pet hairs and loose fibers or dust.

## Easy-to-Clean Surfaces

Countertops in kitchens were traditionally made from wood, and keeping them clean and germ-free was a chore. In 1913, a new material came onto the market, sold under the trade name of Formica. It was made from layers of paper soaked in resin. When heated, the layers made a thin sheet of plastic.

Formica was sold as the "surface with a smile."

Formica did not soak up liquids, it did not attract germs, and it was easy to wipe clean. Because Formica could be printed in colors and patterns, kitchens from the 1940s on were bright and colorful as well as hygienic.

# Time to Spare

As the twentieth century went on, time-saving cleaning products became not just luxuries but necessities. More women worked outside the home and did not have the time to constantly clean the house. While men were not required to help clean the house in the past, they were now expected to do their fair share.

▶ During the late 1900s, men and women shared the housework.

Today we have many labor-saving devices such as handheld vacuum cleaners or vacuum cleaners that can also wash carpets. We have self-cleaning ovens and washing machines that also dry clothes. Household fabrics that are difficult to clean, such as curtains and blankets, can be taken to a drycleaner.

Drycleaners can clean large items in a couple of days.

# Minimal Mess

Traditional Japanese homes are probably the most practical to keep clean. Before people enter a house in Japan, they take off their shoes and leave them by the door. Interiors are open-plan, and furniture is minimal and portable. Even in today's cramped modern apartments, Japanese use foldaway beds and furniture, to make the most of available space.

## Future Improvements

As people become more conscious of air quality, keeping houses dust-free will become increasingly important. It is possible that homes in the future will have garbage-burning furnaces to provide energy. They may have dust-extraction systems to suck dust out of the air before it settles.

Houses may even have lightweight electronic robots to clean windows, floors, and countertops — they could be the servants of the future.

# Timeline

## B.C.
c. 7000    Çatal Hüyük houses built in Mesopotamia.
c. 3000    Skara Brae houses built in Scotland.
c. 500    Ancient Greeks live in homes with courtyards.
c. 200    Romans build aqueducts to supply cities with water.

## A.D.
c. 1300s    Bubonic plague kills one-third of the population of Europe.
1850s    First mechanical dishwasher made in the United States.
1855    The first drycleaner opens in Paris.
1860s    Linoleum first used to cover floors.
1876    American inventor Melville Bissell invents the carpet sweeper.
1880s    First machines for washing clothes at home are made.
1882    William Kent's Rotary Knife Cleaner cleans and sharpens table knives at the same time. First electric iron made.
1901    British inventor Hubert Booth invents the vacuum cleaner.
1906    First electric washing machine invented by Alva Fisher of Chicago.
1907    American James Spangler designs a lightweight vacuum cleaner. He sells his idea to the Hoover Company.
1908    Hoover launches its Model O vacuum cleaner.
1912    First electrically powered dishwasher made.
1913    The Brillo Manufacturing Corporation of New York begins making scouring pads of metal fiber. The Formica Insulation Company of Cincinnati produces Formica.
1917    Nekal, the world's first artificial soap, or detergent, made in Germany.
1921    In Britain, the Unilever Company produces the world's first effective detergent, called Lux.
1926    First electric steam iron, introduced in the United States by the Eldec Company.
1941    World's first aerosol can, containing insect spray, on sale in the United States.
1957    First twin-tub washing machine, housing a washer and a spin-dryer, made.
1967    Proctor & Gamble of Cincinnati creates the world's first biological laundry detergent enriched with enzymes, called Ariel.
1982    Proctor & Gamble creates the world's first liquid detergent for washing machines, called Vizir.

# Glossary

**Anti-macassar** A square of cloth used to protect chairs and sofas.

**Antiseptic** A substance that prevents germs from spreading.

**Aqueduct** A system of canals bringing fresh water into towns.

**Cholera** A disease caught by drinking contaminated water.

**Disinfectant** A substance that kills germs.

**Dolly** Wooden pole used to loosen dirt on clothes while washing.

**Elbow grease** A popular term for hard, manual work.

**Formica** A brand of sheet plastic used to cover surfaces in kitchens.

**Garderobe** A toilet in a castle or large house that empties through a shaft to the outside.

**Hygiene** Making sure things are clean and free of germs.

**Linoleum** A floor covering made from linseed oil, cork, and resin.

**Mangle** A wringing machine for squeezing water out of clothes.

**Mesopotamia** An area now found in the present-day Middle East.

**Middens** Mounds formed when garbage is thrown in one spot.

**Nomads** People who travel constantly and never settle in one place.

**Standpipe** A water pipe, often found at street corners.

**Turpentine** An oil derived from pine trees used in varnish and paint.

# Further Reading

Allen, Eleanor, *Home Sweet Home: A History of Housework*, Dufour, 1979.
Combo, Luann, *Germs (Gross but True series)*, Simon and Schuster, 1997.
Kerr, Daisy, *Keeping Clean (A Very Peculiar History)*, Watts, 1995.
Macdonald, Fiona, *Houses, Habitats and Home Life*, Watts, 1994.

# Index